RIDING ON THE EDGE

Contributors

Editor and Publisher: Geoff Upward, Executive Director, Meadow Brook Estate

Assistant Editor and Researcher: Madelyn Rzadkowolski, Director of Curatorial Services, Meadow Brook Estate

Editorial Coordinator: Ryan Poquette, Veritas Matters

Designer: Lynn Metzker Graphic Design, Davidson, North Carolina

Special thanks to Richard Wilson, Barbara Wilson Eccles, Judy Lavendar, Fredericka and Elizabeth Caldwell, John and Julie Van Lennep and Keith Cupp, publisher of *Bluegrass Horseman,* **for their assistance and contributions.**

On the cover: Frances Dodge at the Devon (Pa.) Horse Show and Country Fair, 1938.

RIDING ON THE EDGE
Frances Dodge and Dodge Stables

BY KAREL BOND LUCANDER

The Meadow Brook Press
Rochester, Michigan

© 2017 by the Meadow Brook Press. All rights reserved.

Published by Meadow Brook Press
350 Estate Drive
Rochester, MI 48309

Printed in the United States of America
Library of Congress Control Number: 2017909093
ISBN 978-1-937086-03-9

In Appreciation

Published with the generous support of John Francis Van Lennep, son of Frances Dodge and grandson of John Francis Dodge and Matilda Rausch Dodge.

Frances Dodge, June 1936. Under her direction, Dodge Stables made a name for itself. As noted in a 1936 edition of Saddle & Bridle, *"Dodge Stables is a place of diversified endeavors, where enthusiasm never lags; it has been built to a position that it is a credit to its owners and about which all of the world might well be proud."*

Contents

Featured Horse Breeds (chart) viii

1 Birth of an auto heiress 1

2 Tragedy and transition 9

3 The equestrian life 17

4 Fame and fashion 25

5 The stamp of Dodge Stables 31

6 Wedding bells 39

7 Loss of a soulmate 45

8 Now *that's* a birthday! 49

9 War hits the circuit 53

10 A team for the ages..59

11 Horse country beckons 69

12 A legacy lives on 75

Featured Horse Breeds

Dodge Stables owned all of these breeds, with the exception of the Thoroughbred, and Wilson Stables owned the Belgians. These horse breeds appear or are referenced throughout the pages that follow.

Average heights in hands (a hand = 4 inches, measured from the withers to the ground) and weights follow the names.

Saddlebred
15-17 hands
900-1,000 lbs.

Lightweight in build with fine-chiseled features; high stepping with exaggerated action. Renowned for having five gaits: walk, trot, canter, slow gait and rack.

Standardbred
14-17 hands
800-1,000 lbs

Best known for its ability in harness racing. Well-muscled, long body, solid legs and powerful shoulders and hindquarters; able to trot or pace at speed for racing.

Belgian
16.2-18 hands
1,800-2,200 lbs.

Descended from the war horse of the Middle Ages. Powerful, heavy muscles and amiable disposition.

Shetland pony
7-10.2 hands
450 lbs.

Intelligent, small size, sturdy build, thick coat, compact and strong.

Hackney pony
12-14.2 hands
1,000 lbs.

Fine, slim, well-proportioned body; long, arched neck; set tail; animated and exaggerated motion.

Thoroughbred
15.2-17 hands
1,000-1,200 lbs.

Tall, slim, athletic, used for racing and other equestrian sports.

November 14, 1914, John (left) and Horace Dodge (middle) introduce their new automobile, a four-door touring car, photographed in front of John's Boston Boulevard home. Identical to this prototype, which they dubbed "Old Betsy," production models would be for sale that day at dealerships throughout the country. The car was priced at $785.

CHAPTER 1

Birth of an auto heiress

Frances Matilda Dodge and her father, John Francis Dodge, November 29, 1918.

On November 27, 1914, a cold, steel gray evening in Detroit, Michigan, John and Matilda Dodge eagerly welcomed their first child, Frances Matilda. Although Frances did not yet know it, she would be given a life of rare privilege and abundant choices as a key figure in the new automotive aristocracy.

Two weeks earlier, John and his brother Horace had taken their first Dodge Brothers car for a spin through the snow-dusted streets of the Motor City – a crowning achievement that was a long time coming. The two worked their way up from humble beginnings in western Michigan and toiled for a decade and a half as machinists in the Detroit and Windsor, Canada, area. This included developing a ball bearing retainer for bicycles that they translated into a successful company, Evans & Dodge Bicycle. In 1900, they sold their interest in that company. The next year, they used the proceeds to open a new machine shop on Beaubien Street in Detroit.

Also in 1901, Ransom Olds hired John and Horace to help manufacture transmissions for his new "curved-dash

John Dodge prepared for his 1907 marriage to 24-year-old Matilda Rausch by constructing a large home in Detroit's most fashionable neighborhood, the Boston-Edison district. The family lived happily there with the three children from John's first marriage, Winifred, Isabel and John Duval. His first wife, Ivy, died of tuberculosis in 1901.

Matilda Rausch as a secretary, c. 1903. Matilda was born in Walkerton, Ontario, on October 19, 1883. Like her husband, she worked her way up from humble beginnings.

John and Matilda Dodge, 1913.

Matilda and Frances Dodge, 1915. Though Frances was a female born into wealth, she was encouraged to make something of herself.

DODGE BROTHERS WORKS - DETROIT

A postcard featuring the Dodge Brothers factory in Hamtramck, c. 1915. As noted in Michigan Manufacturer and Financial Record, *"When the Dodge Bros. car comes out, there is no question that it will be the best thing on the market for the money." Opposite page: Portrait of John Dodge and Horace Dodge, c. 1912. One of John's philosophies, "There is no twilight zone of honesty in business. A thing is right or it's wrong. It's black or it's white."*

Olds" runabout. It was a hefty order, and the brothers worked around the clock, quickly outgrowing their shop space and expanding into a three-story building on Monroe Avenue at Hastings Street. They built a reputation as "the best machinists in Detroit," and others sought out their expertise, including Henry Ford. In 1903, Ford contracted with them to produce running gears for a new car.* When Ford was unable to pay them, they took 10 percent in Ford stock in exchange for parts.

A year earlier, with their company growing from the Olds work, John hired a new secretary, Matilda Rausch. The two married on December 10, 1907. By the time tiny Frances arrived seven years later in 1914, John and his brother Horace had set their sights higher than being parts suppliers, and had formed the Dodge Brothers Motor Car Company.

As Frances entered her toddler years, the fledgling automotive company also quickly found its footing, earning nearly $12 million in net sales in their first seven months (November 1914-June 1915). Their reputation for dependability grew when they fulfilled government orders for Howitzer parts and vehicles during World War I. By the war's end in 1918, the U.S. Army had purchased 13,000 Dodge Brothers cars, more than any other American manufacturer. The next year after a much-publicized conflict, the Dodge brothers sold their Ford Motor Co. stock back to Henry Ford for $25 million, and their own company netted $24 million in sales.

But this good fortune wouldn't last. When Frances was barely 5, in January 1920 during the National Automobile Show in New York City, Horace Dodge contracted the Spanish Influenza. John stayed by Horace's side as he battled the virus. But John, whose lungs were weakened from an earlier bout with tuberculosis, then contracted the flu and died from pneumonia on January 14. Horace would die later that year. Dodge Brothers, in 1920 the second largest producer of automobiles in the United States, had lost its founders. And two families were without their patriarchs.

Dodge Brothers would supply 60 percent of the value of Ford's early models, including the Model T, over the next 10 years.

Above, left to right: Horace, Anna, designer Bloodgood Tuttle, Matilda, Frances and John at the 1918 groundbreaking for John and Matilda's residence in Grosse Pointe, Michigan, purported to be one of the country's largest and just a short distance from Horace and Anna's "Rose Terrace." Left: The Grosse Pointe house under construction in 1920. It would never be completed due to John Dodge's death.

Portrait, c. 1919, of Matilda at age 36, Anna Margaret, an infant (b. 1919), Frances Matilda, age 5 (b. 1914) and Daniel George Dodge, age 2 (b. 1917).

When Frances was born, John Dodge hired Tom Compton as a security guard. Several well-publicized abductions had already struck society's elite and the family staved off their fears by being proactive. After John Dodge's death, Compton became a father figure for the children, especially young Danny. Compton with Frances on a pony (above), c. 1919.

News clipping about John Dodge's death. When John Dodge died, Detroit newspapers lamented that the city would never be the same without the personal attention he paid to the charitable, business and municipal spheres. His young family was equally devastated by the loss.

While staying abroad in Nice, France, the Dodges' elaborately decorated float won the city's Bataille des Fleurs *in 1923. Pictured here are Anna Margaret Dodge, friend Doris Haynes, Matilda, Frances and Danny Dodge.*

CHAPTER 2

Tragedy and transition

Above, left to right: Anna Margaret, Danny and Frances Dodge in costume in Nice, France, 1923.

The family returned to Detroit shocked by John's death and weakened by the flu. Matilda was so sick she had to be carried to his viewing downstairs in their home on East Boston Boulevard.

Once she and her children began to recuperate, questions emerged: What would she do? Where would they live? And there were brewing squabbles over John's colossal estate. He had three older children from his first marriage, and arguments ensued. When legal battles ended in 1922, Matilda was exhausted and ready to retreat far away.

She left for an extended trip to Europe with her and John's children: Frances, Daniel and Anna Margaret. Danny was nearly three years younger than Frances, and younger sister Anna Margaret was just a toddler. Matilda brought along a nurse and a governess, staying for a time at Villa Les Falaises, on the Opal Coast in France. She remained abroad for more than a year, inviting her mother and sister to visit at Christmas. While in Europe, Frances, now 8, was studying French, and Matilda delved into art and architecture.

The family enjoys a casual summer picnic on the grounds of Meadow Brook Farms, c. 1926. Alfred Wilson and Frances are in the foreground. Dan is seated on the left and Matilda the third adult from the left.

When they returned to Michigan, the family moved from their stately East Boston Boulevard mansion into a smaller house on Lincoln Road in Grosse Pointe, not far from her widowed sister-in-law, Anna Thomson Dodge. Yet life would continue to prove shaky. Anna Margaret, 4, contracted the measles and died from an intestinal infection on Palm Sunday, April 13, 1924. Three deaths in four years weighed heavily upon Matilda, Frances and Danny.

Matilda began to think more about the 320-acre farm in Rochester she and John had purchased as newlyweds in 1908 – called Meadow Brook Farm for its windy little creeks, fertile meadows and woodlands. It was John's dream to build a mansion near his brother, Horace, in Grosse Pointe, but also to develop this rural retreat located 20 miles north of the city.

As she continued her life in the Detroit area, Matilda grew closer with a handsome gentleman, Alfred Gaston Wilson. They both attended the First Presbyterian Church. Considered one of the city's most eligible bachelors, Alfred Wilson had never been married and co-owned the successful Wilson Lumber Company with his brother, Donald. Matilda and Alfred became dear friends, and he consoled her through the devastating loss of Anna Margaret.

Alfred would also help keep her grounded when she and her sister-in-law Anna negotiated the sale of the Dodge Brothers Motor Car Company. In May 1925, they struck a deal and sold it to Dillon, Read & Company, a New York investment firm, for $146 million; at the time, the largest cash sale of an American company. This single transaction made Matilda one of the wealthiest women in the world.

Matilda and Alfred were married later that summer on June 29, 1925. When they returned from their British Isles honeymoon, they decided to move the family to Rochester and live in the farmhouse, which she, John and their family had frequented, while building a new residence, Meadow Brook Hall. This 110-room, 88,000-square-foot Tudor Revival-style mansion would take three years and nearly $4 million to complete and furnish. It also featured separate children's wings for Frances

Matilda and Alfred Wilson on their wedding day, June 29, 1925.

In 1926, Matilda and Alfred Wilson began building their 110-room, 88,000-square-foot Tudor Revival residence, Meadow Brook Hall (architect's rendering above). It was the centerpiece of the continually expanding Meadow Brook Farms. Frances had her own wing of the house, which included her bedroom, a guest room and a playroom on the floor above.

When asked why she abandoned the plans to build in Grosse Pointe, Matilda said it was "for the sake of the children." The farm allowed the children to enjoy the pleasures and privacy of rural life.
Above: Frances Dodge with her pony, Lassie, *at Meadow Brook Farms, c. early 1926.*

Frances and Danny ride in a pony cart in front of the Meadow Brook Farms clubhouse, built by their father in 1915. A family guard dog rests nearby, c.1925.

Architectural firm Smith, Hinchman & Grylls designed Frances' playhouse and Bryant & Detwiler constructed it in 1926, the same team that would build Meadow Brook Hall over the next three years. When completed and furnished, Frances' $23,000 fantasy brick house was encircled by a white picket fence (left). The authentic art and accessories that adorned the interior, some imported from Europe, echoed that this was the finest money could buy.

and Danny, each with their own suite of rooms and "hidden" playrooms on the floor above. In addition, the Wilsons had commissioned special playhouses for each child, including a log cabin for Danny and a cottage for Frances, which she received as her 12th year birthday gift.

Originally known as Hilltop Lodge and dubbed "the world's finest doll house" in city and national newspaper headlines, the cottage would eclipse even the fantasy playhouses of other wealthy children at the time, like "million dollar baby" Doris Duke and "poor little rich girls" Barbara Woolworth Hutton and Brenda Frazier. There was nothing to rival this three-quarter scale, six-room brick retreat that was also the first all-electric-powered home of any type in the greater Detroit region. It was eventually renamed Knole Cottage, as its medieval-style architecture was a nod to Knole House, in West Kent, England, where King Henry VIII and Earls and Dukes of Dorset once resided.

Knole Cottage was intended to teach 12-year-old Frances the arts of housekeeping. Above right: Her kitchen featured an electric two-burner cook range, set of tiny pots and pans, jars of jelly, jam and pickles, a small refrigerator, child's drop-leaf oval table with turned legs and a matching tea cart. Right: The cheery pink nursery was a home for a dozen dolls, some the size of old-fashioned matchboxes and others head-to-head with Frances. This room had a cradle, swing and high white dresser for her dolls' dresses, stockings and mittens, even a beaver-trimmed coat.

Frances, 1924, in front of her late father's clubhouse at Meadow Brook Farms. After receiving her first pony at the age of 6, Frances excelled at horsemanship and she began to participate in local and regional horse shows.

CHAPTER 3

The equestrian life

Matilda and Frances at a horse show, c. 1926.

At the age of 6 Frances received a gift that would impact her education and future far more than Knole Cottage would. In 1920 a black-and-white Shetland pony named *King Cole* came to Meadow Brook Farms. Though Frances had ridden ponies before, she loved the joy and independence she felt riding her own pony. Later, Frances injured her hand in a washing wringer accident and her mother encouraged horseback riding as therapy for damaged muscles.

Her interest in horses intensified. In early 1926, Frances and Danny began competing in events at the Detroit Riding and Hunt Club and Grosse Pointe Hunt Club. Soon after, they were showing at the Michigan State Fair. Over the next few years, the family spent weekends traveling to regional horse shows.

Matilda also developed an interest, and now their growing stable included Belgians (with whom Matilda competed successfully against the Budweiser hitch), gaited horses, Shetland ponies, Hackney ponies and Saddlebreds. Especially fond of Saddlebreds, Frances no doubt influenced her parents' decision to build a barn with 24 large box stalls to house new

Though an outdoor riding track and a 24-box-stall barn were constructed just east of Meadow Brook Hall (opposite page), Frances also delighted in riding horses through the woodland paths, meadows and courtyards of the estate. Left: Frances in front of the Gazebo at Meadow Brook Hall, 1931.

Richard, c. 1931.

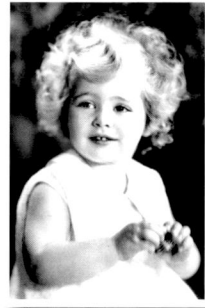

Barbara, c. 1932.

After the Wilsons adopted Richard in 1930, Frances suggested they adopt Barbara in 1931. The baby girl completed the Wilson family.

additions, overseen by trainer Jack Blythe.

By spring 1929, according to newspaper reports, their Meadow Brook Farms stable was "comparing favorably with any in the country," and Frances was "a brilliant young horsewoman." During this whirlwind, Frances, now 15, underwent an appendectomy, but wasn't sidelined long.

Outside the show ring, family life took center stage. In 1930, Matilda and Alfred adopted an infant son, Richard, to Frances' delight. A year later, at Frances' suggestion, they adopted a baby girl, Barbara. These little ones added a new energy to the Dodge-Wilson clan.

As a family, they continued to show and win accolades, including blue ribbons in the fall 1930 Michigan State Fair. By 1931, their stable included a winning pair of Shetland ponies, *Sonny Boy* and *Sonny Girl* (later to become Richard and Barbara's rides), and strikingly matched bay Hackneys, *Buckley Anity* and *Dinarth Sunbeam*.

In May 1932, Frances showed *Pendennis* – her prized Saddlebred – and won at Bradley Farms in New York. On November 5, 1932, Frances and her Saddle Horses first appeared at the National Horse Show in New York City's Madison Square Garden. The world's most famous arena, "The Garden" held the crème de la crème of competitions. Champions *Rosalie Bonheur* and *Pendennis* both took first places there. Back in Rochester, the ponies were now under the watchful eye of manager E.B. "Shine" Ogan.

Frances driving one of her prized Saddlebreds, Pendennis, *c. 1932. According to* Modern Breeds of Livestock, *the American Saddlebred Horse is "the most impressive of all horse breeds, and most people regard it as the most beautiful." Considered "the peacock of the show ring," it has been featured in literature and movies, including* "Black Beauty," "National Velvet," "My Friend Flicka" *and* "Mr. Ed," *the 1960s television show starring a talking horse.*

In June 1933, after graduating from Washington, D.C.'s Mount Vernon Seminary, Frances won double victories at the Michigan State Horse Show. On September 1, at the Ohio State Fair, she took another first with *Pendennis.* As *The Columbus Dispatch* reported: *"Much of his success was due no doubt to the proficient horsemanship of Miss Dodge."* The tack room now boasted more than 100 blue ribbons.

But the stable would suffer a major blow on October 6, when *Dinarth Sunbeam* was fatally stricken with a cold, breaking up America's most famous Hackney team.

Even while grieving for *Sunbeam,* Frances continued competing. For the October World's Fair Horse Show in Chicago, Frances entered the largest string of equine blue bloods – shipping 14 horses by rail from Detroit to the Windy City's 124th Field Artillery Armory. She would ride and drive all of them, taking first in the Shetland pony class and pocketing five first-place wins in the Saddle classes.

On November 9, 1933, Frances took one of the most important prizes at the National Horse Show in New York, riding *Anita Rose.* By early December, she returned home triumphant from the Toronto Horse Show and

Left: 1936 Portrait of Frances at age 18 atop one of her favorite Saddlebred show horses, Pendennis, *with Pekingese,* Robyne, *by artist George Ford Morris. Morris set the gold standard for equine paintings.*

Frances and her horses were receiving much positive press, as on this cover of The Rider And Driver, *1932.*

International Show in Chicago. According to the December 10, 1933, *Detroit Times,* "*At both shows every one of her entries emerged with a ribbon, though she was pitted against the best show horses on the continent.*"

After a bittersweet season, during which she collected dozens of blue ribbons but lost one of her favorite animals, Frances set aside the reins for her debutante ball.

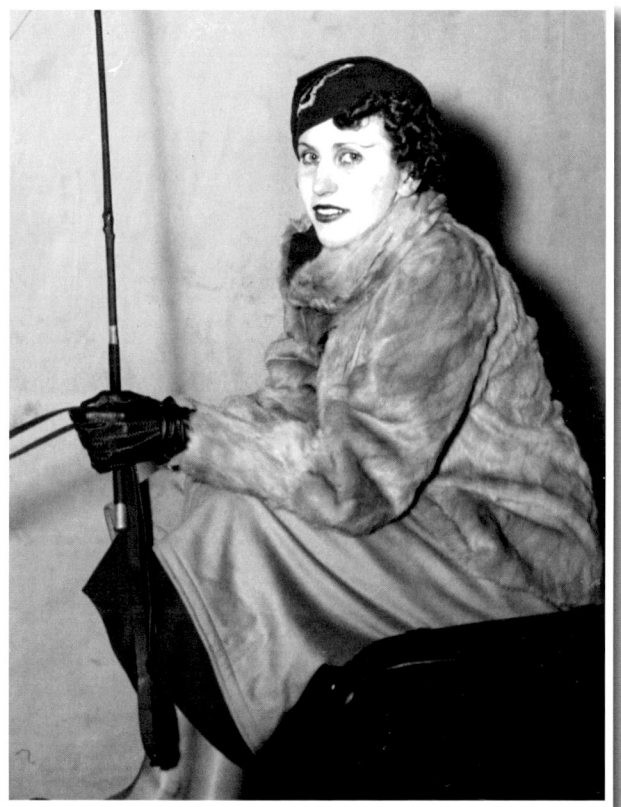

Frances won five blue ribbons at the National Horse Show at Madison Square Gardens in 1933. At only 18 years old she tied for third place in the civilian category.

When not on the show circuit, Frances enjoyed the Meadow Brook estate; here at the clubhouse garden, 1932.

Matilda, Frances and Alfred at Detroit's Book-Cadillac Hotel for her debutante ball, December 1933. When the Book brothers built the luxurious Book-Cadillac Hotel in 1923, it cost $14 million to construct. When it opened in December 1924, this 33-story Neo-Renaissance beauty was the tallest hotel in the world. Until Frances, the season's wealthiest deb, held her party there, the Book-Cadillac had not been the venue for such a posh soiree since 1928, before the Great Depression began. As reported in the Detroit Times, *"Somehow it is a sure sign that prosperity has returned."*

CHAPTER 4

Fame and fashion

Frances Dodge, 1933.

In her spare moments between training and horse shows, 19-year-old Frances Dodge was preparing to make her bow to society. On Wednesday, December 27, 1933, at 10 p.m., a steady stream of some 600 well-heeled guests exited limos, pulled mink capelets around their shoulders, adjusted tuxedos and made their way into the chic Book-Cadillac Hotel for Frances' coming out party. Guests were still arriving even after midnight, among them the 27 other Detroit debutantes of the season.

As her guests entered, they found ballrooms awash in hundreds of silver balloons, mirrored spheres, swaths of black and silver fabric, ice sculptures and black and silver eucalyptus trees. Such cotillions usually featured great blossoms of alabaster, and debutantes dressed in white gowns, white gloves and white pearls. But Frances Dodge – exhibiting the independent air that characterized her show ring and business acumen – bucked convention, wearing a silver gown and sandals and a tiara of black feathers. When the specially ordered black orchid corsage did not arrive,

Above, left: Before her debut in 1933, Frances took a formal bow to society at her family home. Publicity shots were taken of her in a velvet gown with silver fingernails. Right: After her coming out ball, Frances' six-month cross-continental trip – a treat to her parents – received lots of press, including the account above. Their tour included a 20-day cruise of the West African coast and an 18-day automobile tour of Spain and North Africa.

Frances dyed a single stem with shoe polish and carried it through the night.

A sumptuous supper buffet, including Vermont turkey, whole roasted ham, sunburst salad and biscuit tortoni, was served at 1 a.m. In the background, two orchestras played the latest jazz and swing hits until 5 a.m.

This $25,000 event – five times what it cost to build a new house in the early '30s and about $460,000 in today's dollars – was talked about for decades.

Following her debutante party, Frances, the girl-turning-woman, yearned to see wild, untamed places like those she had read about in *The Arabian Nights* and the works of Rudyard Kipling. Knowing she would soon receive her inheritance from her late father's estate, she treated her parents, Matilda and Alfred, to a spectacular cross-continental journey. On January 20, 1934, they boarded the *Conte Di Savoia*, gliding along for stops in Morocco, equatorial Africa, Egypt, India and Europe. During their

Frances, Matilda and Alfred in Egypt, 1934.

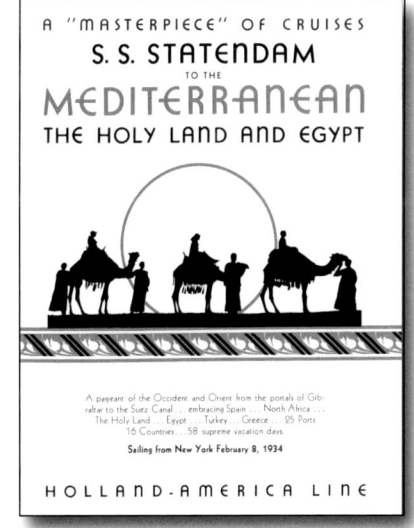

Matilda, Alfred and Frances aboard an elephant in India, 1934. In letters to friends, Frances would describe how "The Taj Mahal takes your breath away, no matter how many times you have seen pictures of its beauty." One of their last city visits in India was to Darjeeling, where they drank their morning coffee watching the sunrise over Mt. Everest in nearby Nepal.

six-month excursion, they would visit 58 cities and cover 33,048 miles.

Competing newspapers hummed about this trip, considered unorthodox, even among the jet set: *"Wealthiest Deb Starts on Trip Which She Herself Planned Out; Hopes to Meet Real Sheik on Her Travels"* read the headline in the January 19 *Detroit Times*.

Upon her return in late July, Frances brought back 36 new horses, four donkeys, one zebra (a second died in transit), two large African leopard tortoises, and five rare white and two white-and-black Pekingese from England. She also hired Mrs. G.R. Watson, licensed English kennel-maid, to properly train her exotic new purebreds. Shortly after returning, Frances had an elaborate kennel built for the dogs and comfortable quarters for Mrs. Watson.

This unusual collection of animals invited more attention from the press, who were never far from Frances. As reported "In Mayfair with The Chaperon," July 20, 1934, *Detroit Times*: *"Most girls would arrive home with gowns galore from Paris … curiously shaped bottles of expensive and thoroughly divine perfumes … But not Frances! Instead, she returns to us with a veritable menagerie!"*

Now back home at Meadow Brook, Frances didn't take long to rest before she turned her attention back to her first love … horses.

Two of the Pekingese puppies Frances brought back from England in 1934. Once home, she built a lavish kennel complex to house these purebreds, including a showroom, fully equipped kitchen, bathing area, infirmary and living quarters for the kennelmaid she hired in England, G. Ruby Watson (above). When Ruby fell ill in 1957, Frances provided her and the remaining dogs with a furnished home in Rochester.

Frances with her many winning ribbons from the National Horse Show, November 1936. According to the prescient American Horseman Sportologue, *May 1936: "When the history of the 1936 Horse Show is written, there is hardly any doubt that one of its most important chapters will be devoted to that outstanding string from the stable of Miss Frances M. Dodge of Rochester, Michigan ... For real showmanship, expert reinsman ability and true sportsmanship, Miss Dodge deserves the blue ribbon. She is as modest in her conquests as she is game in her defeats."*

CHAPTER 5

The stamp of Dodge Stables

By 1935, now 20, Frances owned 80 horses, and she and her mother continued to enter horse shows together. As Frances began to win more prizes and recognition, "Miss Dodge," as the equestrian world referred to her, set her sights on more significant accomplishments. She had developed a knack for pursuing the best-bred equines to add to her already award-winning stock. And she had the means to do it.

With her stepfather Alfred's help, Frances was traveling thousands of miles to handpick the royalty of stables and horse centers throughout the United States and across the Atlantic, including English Hackney country. Meadow Brook's harness division manager, Shine Ogan, would also go on short trips to Missouri, Tennessee and Kentucky, looking over prospective show horses to add. The thoroughness with which Frances chose stock gave her burgeoning and newly named "Dodge Stables" an edge. Frances was not

Dodge Stables letterhead.

Frances Dodge purportedly spent $100,000 building a new stables complex in 1934-35. The new "Dodge Stables" buildings dominated the landscape of the now 1,500-acre Meadow Brook Farms as well as the equestrian world. Its award-winning breeding program bred both Saddlebreds and Hackney ponies from the finest stock in the world. The two stables buildings at the left (the one at far left the original 24-stall structure) connected to a 23,000-square-foot riding/show ring, complete with a large second-floor observation room that boasted trophy cases, a wet bar and men's and women's dressing rooms and bathrooms. Matilda and Alfred's "Wilson Stables" is the building at the far right. Meadow Brook Hall can be seen in the upper left background.

Horses from Dodge Stables, as well as Frances herself, were regularly featured in Saddle & Bridle, American Horseman *and* The American Weekly. *Above: Cover photo of Frances and Hackney ponies* Sweet Melody *and* Avon Swell *from* Saddle & Bridle *magazine, 1935.*

PHOTO COURTESY OF CALDWELL FAMILY

only interested in claiming ribbons at competitions, but also in creating bloodlines considered the best by the standards of the country's horse capital, Lexington, Kentucky, and even by world standards.

In addition, Frances oversaw construction in 1934-35 of new state-of-the-art barns, stables and paddocks, including a nearly 23,000-square-foot indoor riding ring for winter conditioning. Frances also hired a man at the top of his game, Wallace Bailey, to serve as Saddle Horse stable manager.

All this work paid off, and the elite horses of the new Dodge Stables continued to rack up awards at high-profile horse shows. Shetland ponies *High Tension* and *Star Dust* were becoming an invincible pair and were champions at the International Livestock show in Chicago. Frances also had a winning Three-Gaited mare, *Society Barrymore*, who had firmly established herself as one of the best of the over-15.2 hands division. She added another Three-Gaited mare, *Etta Kett*, whose first year's record included 11 blue ribbons. Both had strong bloodlines and would make valuable broodmares when they were retired from the show ring.

In April 1935, after scouring the country for top Five-Gaited horses, Frances followed Bailey's recommendation and won acclaimed show gelding *As Thousands Cheer* in a bidding war. The sale was reported to be nearly $25,000, one of the largest sums paid up to that time for a horse.

Above: Dodge Stables' expert Hackney trainer, Reed Bridgford, driving champion King of the Plain.
PHOTO COURTESY OF BRIDGFORD FAMILY

Left: Frances, 1936.

MISS FRANCES M. DODGE
Owner of
Frances M. Dodge Stables
ROCHESTER, MICH.

Miss Dodge is the daughter of Mr. and Mrs.
A. G. Wilson, of Rochester

Frances and King of the Plain *at Madison Square Garden, New York, 1936.*

As noted in the June 1935 issue of *The Kentucky Horseman,* "*As Thousands Cheer* carries the blood of champions and is a brilliant horse in action … It is predicted that long before the season of 1935 is ended, many will call him cheap at that price." At the subsequent Newark, New Jersey, event, *As Thousands Cheer* swept the awards.

As Dodge Stables grew, Frances also made some shrewd staffing decisions, including replacing harness manager Shine Ogan with Reed Bridgford, who had years of experience showing and fine-tuning Hackneys and ponies.

In Atlantic City, New Jersey, in May 1935, Frances attended "The Olympic of America," a spectacular historical exhibition that emulated medieval England. It was the first horse show of its kind, and Dodge Stables monopolized the awards, including top showings for *Society Barrymore, Etta Kett* and *As Thousands Cheer.*

After The Olympic fanfare, Frances invested in another star performer, *Shalimar.* This British import was predicted to become one of the country's greatest heavy harness horses. He won 18 championships or reserves and 54 blues in England before she brought him to Rochester. His first appearance with Frances was the 1935 Devon Show in Philadelphia, where he made quite an impression. Tom Clark, one of the country's best show managers and judges, prompted onlookers to "watch that chestnut. The Dodge

DINARTH SUNBEAM & BUCKLEY ANITY

Christmas morning did not begin at Meadow Brook until Frances arrived at the front door in a sleigh filled with presents for the family (pictured here, c. 1932). One year, as they moved the presents under the tree in the grand living room, Frances led a horse in, a present for her mother. The surprise delighted young Richard and Barbara. Below: Barbara and Richard Wilson with their ponies, Midget *and* Tom Tit, *and their spaniel,* Sandy, *c. 1934.*

gelding." Though *Shalimar* didn't take Devon by storm that year, he would return to show them what he was made of.

Despite all the new and exciting champions being added to her stable, Frances again suffered a devastating loss. Much-trumpeted star, *As Thousands Cheer*, died at the Detroit show in July. Though his cause of death was not reported, *As Thousands Cheer* had contracted a virus that hit the equine world in 1935 and he may have succumbed to that. His passing struck a somber note, and gave notice that good fortune would not always smile upon Dodge Stables – or Frances and her family.

Throughout the mid-1930s, Frances and Dodge Stables continued to make headlines with her horse acquisitions and wins, including the 1936 Devon Horse Show, where *Shalimar* took first place in the harness division championship. *"There is a saying that a fourth at Devon is better than a blue elsewhere,"* according to *Turf and Tanbark*. That year and the following, 1937, Frances' entries won the highest number of points in the show, and she was twice presented with the silver Devon Victory Challenge Cup.

Another new addition to the Stables, *King of the Plain* ("monarch of the Hackney field"), seemed to hold court wherever he was shown. This little stallion remained undefeated for several years. In the hands of Reed Bridgford, *King* seemed to win stakes wherever he touched ground.

Back home in Rochester, Frances' young siblings, Richard and Barbara, were favoring their 29-inch ponies, *Tom Tit* and *Midget*, with a lot of hugs. It was a sweet reminder that Frances and her family's relationship with their animals went far beyond counting wins and headlines.

Much to Frances' displeasure, the media also followed her relentlessly beyond the horse shows. One of the country's richest young ladies, she remained a curiosity. If she painted her fingernails white, or slipped away early from a party to White Tower for some "Wimpy Specials," the 5-cent mini hamburgers she had a weakness for, a story would appear in one of Detroit's three daily newspapers, if not all of them. Whatever she did was scrutinized and picked apart.

This was especially true when it came to her love of fashion, where no detail was too obscure for the press. In the August 5, 1934, edition of the *Detroit Times*, reporter Minnie Cage cornered Frances about the favorite pieces in her wardrobe. Frances obligingly replied: *"I'm torn between a black and white afternoon gown and a black evening gown. The afternoon gown is very long and has a high waist. It's a Chanel model. The evening gown is of black horsehair lace. It's quite different from any other dress I've ever seen."*

Yet for Frances, if there were a showdown between fashion and horses, horses won hands down. Horses were her passion, and they would soon also ignite a new love.

Frances, Jimmy Johnson and her parents greet their wedding guests in Meadow Brook Hall's library, including Clara Ford (in print dress) and Henry Ford (in white linen), foreground. Ford had subcontracted Frances' father, John Dodge, and uncle, Horace Dodge, to help manufacture running gears for his cars before they would found Dodge Brothers Motor Car Company in 1914.

CHAPTER 6

Wedding bells

Frances in her ice-blue silk satin wedding gown holding a bouquet of orchids and lilies of the valley.

James B. ("Jimmy") Johnson, Jr., had become a familiar face to Frances at horse shows throughout the country. A journalist who covered the equestrian beat, Johnson was kind, had an outgoing, jovial personality and a fun, yet hard-working spirit. He complemented Frances, whose shyness sometimes masked her good humor and loving nature. She first met Jimmy when she was 18 and he was 27, at the National Horse Show in New York City. They shared a common passion that took the lion's share of their time and thoughts: horses.

They announced their engagement on Sunday, May 22, 1938, in a novel way. Some 30 friends were invited to a supper buffet at Meadow Brook Hall. There, on the banquet table, were two flower rings with glass bowls holding yellow, diamond-shaped flowers. Frances' and James' initials were linked together in one bowl, and Dan's initials were linked with his fiancée, Laurine MacDonald, in the second bowl. So not one, but two of "the Dodge kids" would soon be tying the knot. As Dan wrote in the guest book, "The

Frances with her wedding party. Aside from the maid of honor, Miss Nancy Smith, who wore rose taffeta, they all wore dresses in shades of blue, from pale ceil to deep lapis. In addition to receiving these custom-made Peggy Hoyt gowns, Frances presented her attendants with diamond and platinum brooches. Other well-wishers included the nearly 100 farm and Hall employees who took a break from their duties to watch their beloved Frances walk down the aisle.

Frances and Jimmy's five-layer, 3-foot-high wedding cake. Each guest would leave the reception with a piece of cake individually boxed with white satin ribbon and tulle with a sprig of waxed orange blossom.

Greatest Day in All History of Meadowbrook Hall."

Frances' wedding came first. On Friday, July 1, nearly 500 guests arrived at Meadow Brook Hall for Frances and James' wedding festivities. The family and close friends were led to the living room, where the exchange of vows took place in front of the large carved-oak fireplace.

As the house's massive Aeolian pipe organ swung into Lohengrin's *Wedding March,* the wedding party filed in. On the arm of Dan, Frances followed, stunning in a Grecian-style ice-blue satin gown. The gown's bodice was encrusted with blue seed pearls and the scalloped train extended four-and-a-half yards. Her tiara tulle veil was also ice blue, and she held a bouquet of rare white cattleya orchids, white spray butterfly orchids and lilies of the valley. "Detroit's No. 1 Glamour Girl" – a title reflective of her extravagant and original ideas of dress – lived up to her reputation that night.

After a simple exchange of vows, guests feasted on French salmon, creamed chicken in patty shells, veal aspic and steaming scallops, lobster and shrimp salads, and cold meats. A meringue baked in wedding rose moulds and filled with ice cream served as dessert. The 3-foot-high wedding cake, frosted in a calla lily design, was centered on the Belgian lace-covered table and crowned with an arrangement of spathiphyllum and lilies of the valley.

FRANCES DODGE BRIDE ON FRIDAY

HEIRESS SPEAKS VOWS AT HOME NEAR ROCHESTER

WEARS ICE BLUE SATIN

A bridal gown of classic inspiration was worn by Miss Frances M. Dodge for her wedding to James B. Johnson, Jr., of Elizabeth, N. J. Friday evening at Meadow Brook Hall, the home of her mother, Mrs. Alfred G. Wilson, near Rochester.

Gown of Ice Blue Satin

Miss Dodge selected a gown, Grecian in its simplicity and designed of endless yards of ice blue satin. The bodice is moulded to the waistline with an embroidered motif of encrusted pearls of ice blue colorings, the design of acanthus leaves. The skirt extends into a scalloped train more than four yards long. A filmy veil of ice blue illusion is bound and scalloped with satin bindings, and surmounted by a tiara of ice blue illusion encrusted with ice blue seed pearls. She carried white orchids.

The ceremony took place at 8:30 o'clock in the living room in front of the mantle which was banked with white flowers. Candelabra were the only adornments on the mantle. Dr. Joseph A. Vance of Detroit read the service and Miss Dodge was given in marriage by her brother, Daniel G. Dodge.

Miss Nancy Smith of Detroit was maid of honor and wore a dress of pale rose taffeta souffle. The bodice has a square decolletage surmounted by a taffeta and tulle bow. The bouffant skirt, bias draped, extends into a short train. Her flowers were gardenias.

Bridesmaids were Miss Constance Kelly, of Sioux City, Ia.; Miss Laurine MacDonald of Gore Bay, Ont., fiancee of the bride's brother; Miss Virginia Johnson of Elizabeth, N. J.; Mrs. Lewis Cedargreen of Detroit and Mrs. Lewis F. Brown of Detroit.

MRS. JAMES B. JOHNSON, JR.

Mr. and Mrs. Johnson will sail from New York City for a honeymoon in England on the Bremen tonight. Before her marriage Friday evening at the home of her mother, Mrs. Alfred G. Wilson, near Rochester, Mrs. Johnson was Miss Frances M. Dodge, noted horsewoman and society leader.

"It wasn't our mutual interest for swing music that brought Frances and me together. I first met her at the National Horse Show in New York in November of 1933. And later that night we danced together at the horse show ball." Detroit Evening Times, *May 24, 1938, quoting Jimmy. After years of seeing each other at horse shows, Frances and Jimmy's friendship blossomed into romance. Above: Frances' wedding featured in the* Pontiac (Mich.) Daily Press, *July 2, 1938.*

As the receiving line set up in the library, a local six-piece swing band, "the Sophistocats," played on a specially constructed "under the stars" dance floor below the stone terrace on Meadow Brook's south lawn, so the hundreds of guests could take in the summer air while dancing the night away.

A month later, after returning from their honeymoon tour through the British countryside, the new Mr. and Mrs. Johnson settled into the old farmhouse on the Meadow Brook estate.

Above: Jimmy and Frances, c. 1942. Right: Jimmy and Frances with friends at a horse show, the caption reading, "The Satisfied Exhibitors," c. 1943.

PHOTO COURTESY OF JUDY LAVENDAR

Frances and brother Dan competing together at the Cleveland Way in 1929. Four years later, Dan abandoned the horse circuit to pursue his interests in the outdoors and machining, with Frances telling reporters, "[Dan] isn't very interested in horses. He spends all the time he can with boats and tinkering and mechanics."

CHAPTER 7

Loss of a soulmate

Dan walks Frances down Meadow Brook Hall's grand staircase on her wedding day. The lifelong bond and understanding between them would soon be forever severed.

Almost a month to the day after Frances became Mrs. Johnson, Dan Dodge married Annie "Laurine" MacDonald, daughter of a Canadian boat captain. Dan disliked large, formal events, so they were wed in a simple ceremony August 2, 1938, in Meadow Brook's Breakfast Room. Attendants included Laurine's sister and brother-in-law, Leona and Frederick G. Holmes.

Dan, who had inherited his father's interests in mechanical tinkering and exploring and enjoying the outdoors, knew just where to take his new bride for their honeymoon. They headed to the place they had first met and fell in love: Manitoulin Island, a near-wilderness sanctuary in Lake Huron in the province of Ontario.

Laurine had grown up on the island and was its telephone operator. Dan had purchased the 600-acre estate on Maple Point, complete with a comfortable log hunting lodge, when he was only 16. The lodge was a half-hour ride out on the jagged and winding peninsula road from Kagawong, the largest town on the island.

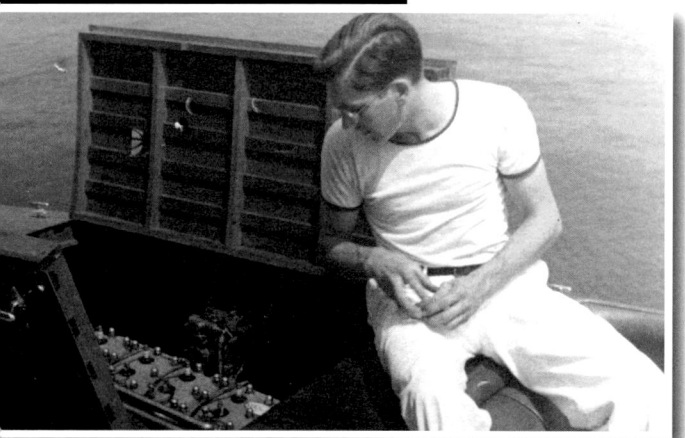

Top left: Alfred, Matilda, Frances and Dan at the Meadow Brook Hall groundbreaking, 1926. Above, Laurine and Dan Dodge on their wedding day, 1938. Left: Dan tinkering on his boat, c. 1936.

On August 15, two weeks into the honeymoon, their trip went awry. Dan, Laurine and two caretakers were injured when old sticks of dynamite that Dan was testing unexpectedly exploded. Though accounts are sketchy, they chose Dan's speedboat to reach medical assistance faster than the overland route would have allowed. The waves were extremely choppy, and as Dan stood to try to help Laurine steer, he fell overboard. After feverishly searching for him, his stunned wife and companions continued toward the hospital to get help for those who were injured.

Though a sizable reward was offered by the Wilsons to find him, it wasn't until 23 days later that two fishermen discovered his body. A coroner's jury found the death accidental. Laurine contested the $250,000 she was given in the prenuptial agreement and after a four-year dispute with the family, settled for $2.5 million.

The loss of this young Dodge heir, with dark hair and steel-rimmed spectacles, mechanical gifts and a gentle spirit, would leave a huge void in the hearts of his family, particularly his older sister and his mother. After he was laid to rest, Matilda closed his wing in The Hall and his Meadow Brook cabin, and kept them locked for many years.

Frances was in shock. He was her beloved brother, the one who had endured alongside her the death of their younger sister and their father, the legendary John Dodge. He was her touchstone, her confidant, her biological link to the future … and now he was gone.

Frances rushed home when she heard the news of Dan's tragic accident.

Frances posing during a party at Meadow Brook Hall, 1933. Dubbed "Detroit's No. 1 Glamour Girl" during her debut season in 1933, Frances retained that title after her 1938 marriage. Detroit nightclubs buzzed with approval at each satin, lamé or lace gown Frances wore as she swirled around the dance floor to the newest and wildest music of the day: swing. She and husband Jimmy used their influence to support local and national bands. By hiring them for private events and name-dropping in newspaper interviews, Detroit's swing music scene was on the rise.

CHAPTER 8

Now *that's* a birthday!

Meadow Brook Hall dining room set for Frances' 25th birthday dinner. She did not know that 150 friends and her favorite swing music band had gathered for a surprise in the nearby ballroom.

A year after her brother's passing, Frances was preparing for a major milestone in her life. On her 25th birthday, November 27, 1939, she would officially inherit a $10 million trust fund from the John Dodge estate.

She intended to celebrate the occasion with a quiet dinner at her parents' home. However, as she left Meadow Brook's formal Christopher Wren dining room, Frances heard "Happy Birthday" erupt from below. The gallery windows overlooked the two-story ballroom, giving Frances the perfect vantage point to see one of her favorite musicians, Tommy Dorsey, and his 22-piece orchestra, set up to entertain the 150 other guests that Matilda and Frances' husband Jimmy had invited and directed to slip quietly into the ballroom.

The Johnsons were aficionados of swing and were friends of Dorsey's. As a return favor for letting him borrow the Wilsons' plane in a pinch, he traveled with his band from Chicago to give Frances a rousing surprise performance. A young backup singer – Frank Sinatra – accompanied the famous Dorsey when the lead singer unexpectedly fell ill.

Frances and her husband, Jimmy Johnson, were fans of swing music as well as supporters of local and national musicians. Jimmy served as editor of Cats Meow, *the guide to swing music. This premiere edition, May 1938, would have been produced around the time of their marriage, when his office adjoined the Wilsons' Detroit business offices in the Fisher Building. Jimmy and Frances became followers of, and friends with, many of the bands they researched for the magazine, including the Tommy Dorsey Band. Bandleaders Hal Kemp and Tommy Dorsey sent wires congratulating the couple on their nuptials in 1938. Reading them, Frances said, "I think that's darned sweet, Jimmy." Left: Blue and metallic gold evening gown worn by Frances Dodge, c. 1936.*

Already making waves as a lead, Sinatra was on his way up the celestial ladder. The evening was a huge success, and two months later Sinatra made his first public appearance with Tommy Dorsey and his orchestra.

Swing became popular in the early 1930s for its lilting rhythm, excitable solos by talented musicians, and most of all its danceable tunes. Though it was a sound that did not typically appeal to the older generation, Frances' close-knit family would not miss the chance to celebrate her 25th birthday. Her parents and uncle Don and aunt Mabel Wilson, with their sons Don Jr. and Oliver, joined the crowd. Siblings 10-year-old Richard and 8-year-old Barbara didn't miss the fun, either. They were allowed to stay up late and watch the flurry of dancing from the gallery windows that overlooked the two-story ballroom. At one point, Tommy Dorsey called out for Richard to name the next song they would play. With little background in popular music, Richard replied with the only song he could think of: "Home on the Range!"

At midnight, the guests gathered for a buffet supper in the dining room. A brilliantly lit birthday cake was brought in and the "who's who" of Detroit enjoyed a night to remember.

Frances was not distracted by the party for long; the following weekend, she and Jimmy left for the International Horse Show in Chicago and their last show of the decade. Though Frances' operation saw enormous growth in the 1930s – most particularly with the establishment and development of Dodge Stables – her successes in the 1940s would catapult her into equestrian history.

While Frances and Jimmy bonded over a love of horses, they also enjoyed jazz and swing music. They were equally happy together on the family farm, dancing to live music in Detroit's hottest clubs, and at horse shows (above, c. 1939).

Frances with daughter Judy on pony Num Num *at Meadow Brook Hall, c. 1942.*

PHOTO COURTESY OF JUDY LAVENDAR

CHAPTER 9

War hits the circuit

Frances presents an award to a cavalry officer, c. 1943.

PHOTO COURTESY OF JUDY LAVENDAR

The Nazis rolled into Poland on Sept. 1, 1939, and the ripples of a new war would soon wash up on American soil. By 1940, the country was still feeling the effects of the Great Depression, United States debt was reaching its highest level to date and the average annual household income was about $1,300.

Though Meadow Brook Hall was completed two weeks before the Great Depression began, the property continued to flourish. The young and vibrant Frances especially brought life to her family's American country estate. She, along with husband Jimmy Johnson, insulated by their wealth, began new construction projects and business ventures, including expanding Dodge Stables. In Rochester during the 1930s, Meadow Brook Farms was considered one of the best places to find steady employment.

The Johnsons continued acquiring champions and Frances continued riding and winning accolades, including a world record for trotting under saddle at The Red Mile racetrack in Kentucky on September 27, 1940.

While growing their stables and reputation, the Johnsons

Mrs. Frances Dodge Johnson, riding Greyhound (1.55¼ to sulky) to his sensational world's record of 2:01¾ for a mile under saddle

Although not owned by Frances Johnson, Standardbred gelding Greyhound *was the trotting horse of his day. Above left: On September 27, 1940, at the Red Mile racetrack in Lexington, Kentucky, Frances set a new world's mile record of 2:01-3/4 for a trotter under saddle, riding* Greyhound. *They flew around the track, with* Greyhound's *trainer and regular driver, Sep Palin, alongside driving a Thoroughbred hooked to a sulky. The record stood for 54 years and was later broken by* Moni Maker, *a mare bred by Frances' daughter Rikki, and ridden by jockey Julie Krone. Above right: photo taken that day in 1940.*

PHOTO COURTESY OF KEITH CUPP, BLUEGRASS HORSEMAN

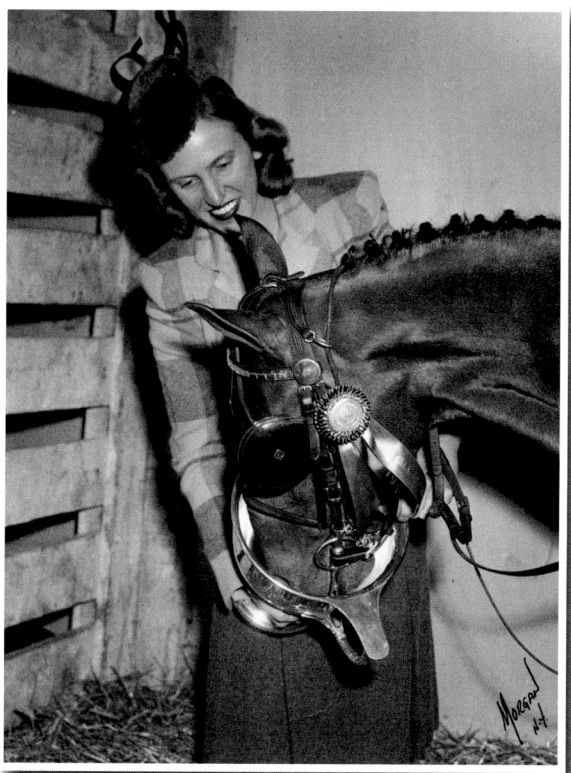

Frances serves her winning Hackney pony from a silver trophy cup, 1941.
PHOTO COURTESY OF JUDY LAVENDAR

also began to expand their family. Exactly three years to the day they were married, on July 1, 1941, Jimmy and Frances welcomed a baby daughter, Judith Frances Johnson, to Meadow Brook Farms.

Outside of the Wilsons' and Johnsons' country retreat, the reverberations of World War II were impacting horse shows. On the morning of December 7, 1941, as the Imperial Japanese Navy bombed Pearl Harbor, Hawaii, the annual Chicago International Horse Show was already underway. Frances was in attendance with her charges, and as the news was broadcast, a deathly silence fell over the arena. There were no clip-clopping hooves, no announcers talking, and no riders discussing strategies … only the sounds of horses' tails swishing.

According to an account in *American Saddlebred*: *"In 1942, many horse shows, including the Kentucky State Fair, were cancelled for war-related reasons, such as gas rationing and use of facilities by the military. The horse industry united to reopen events for public morale; there was even a congressional hearing to get steel for making horseshoe nails."*

Despite the effects of war, and Jimmy Johnson joining the Army Air Corps, the Dodge Stables' Hackneys and Saddle Horses still appeared on the circuit, and continued to make waves in the horse world. In particular, Dodge Stables' head Saddle stallion, *Anacacho Shamrock*, showed strong,

"Mrs. Johnson, one of the country's leading horsewomen and whips, rides and drives in many of the shows, and this year was no exception."
– Saddle & Bridle, *December 1942.* Left: Frances, July 1943, watching new trainer Sep Palin driving **Worthy Boy** *in Cleveland, Ohio. Lt. James B. Johnson served in the Army Air Corps during World War II. Before moving to Michigan, Jimmy served in the Essex troop, an elite cavalry group in the New Jersey National Guard.*

PHOTO BELOW COURTESY OF JUDY LAVENDAR

Frances drives a carriage with soldiers playfully overfilling the bench seat, c. 1945, at Dodge Stables' winter home in Aiken, South Carolina. Jimmy enjoyed playing polo, golf and riding hunters there but Frances was not a fan. Frances and Jimmy rented a property in Aiken until deciding to move the entire operation to Lexington, Kentucky.

PHOTO COURTESY OF JUDY LAVENDAR

consistent form and great speed. Still young, he was also a promising sire. Frances hired *Greyhound's* former trainer, Sep Palin, who brought his expertise and penchant for success.

Dodge Stables had a good year, and the horse industry looked ahead to happier times. *Saddle & Bridle* editor Arthur Van Ronzelen summed up the state of affairs in his December 1942 edition: "Breed your show mares of today, and be ready for a glorious era when the Angel of Peace has come again to dwell among us … Breeding now assumes the most important role in the horse world today. It will be our way of carrying on."

Little did anyone know that by the time Van Ronzelen wrote this, Dodge Stables was already doing its part. In four months, an exceptional colt would be born into a tumultuous world, soon to make his own headlines.

Portrait of Earl Teater atop Wing Commander *(by George Ford Morris).*
"*The story of the decade, other than the war, was the rise of CH* Wing
Commander, *the first horse to win six World's Grand Championships.
In an era of formidable show horses,* Wing *stood alone, heading the
increasingly powerful Dodge Stables' show string. By the 1950s, the
rallying cry at horse shows across the country would be, 'Beat Dodge!'*"
– American Saddlebred, *November/December 1999.*

PHOTO COURTESY OF KEITH CUPP, *BLUEGRASS HORSEMAN*

CHAPTER 10

A team for the ages

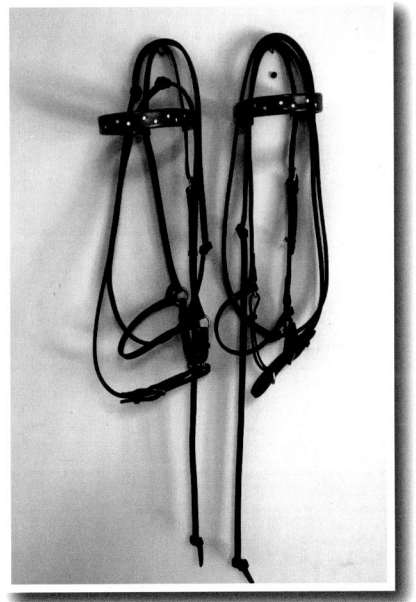

Dodge Stables weanling show bridles from the Bluegrass Horseman *collection, c. 1940.*

PHOTO COURTESY OF KEITH CUPP, *BLUEGRASS HORSEMAN*

To breed champions, Dodge Stables had been cherry picking from among the world's finest horses, including the prized mare *Flirtation Walk*. Saddle horse stable manager Wallace Bailey had also snapped up champion stallion *Anacacho Shamrock* after observing him at the Golden Gate International Championship.

In 1941, *Flirtation Walk* was first bred to *Anacacho Shamrock*, producing a filly, Lover's Lane. On April 23, 1943, *Flirtation Walk* then gave birth to *Wing Commander*, also sired by *Anacacho Shamrock*. Wallace Bailey kept a close eye on this little colt he called *"Wing."*

Along with these new additions, Bailey was also carefully grooming other new mares and stallions to garner top trophies, and hired Bill Rowan and brothers Joe and Gregory Peña to help with *Anacacho* and *Wing* respectively.

But all the progress would abruptly stop.

During the 1944 holidays, Bailey fell ill and spent four days in the hospital before dying unexpectedly and tragically on Christmas Eve. More than 100 people

Dodge Stables' barn in Rochester, Michigan, where Wing Commander *was foaled April 23, 1943. He was out of* Flirtation Walk *and sired by* Anacacho Shamrock. *His powerful, well-bred magic was not haphazard, and* Wing *(not pictured here) would not need much coaxing to acquire a taste for blue ribbons once he began competing.*

attended his funeral in the Dodge Stables riding ring, including a young Richard Wilson. His passing left a large personal void for Frances, but also a quandary. Wallace Bailey had brought Dodge Stables so far, who could possibly fill his boots?

Earl Teater was a man who knew how illness could turn lives upside-down. Growing up on a farm in Kentucky in the 1910s, both his parents suddenly became sick. Earl was the second of eight children, and he and his older brother Lloyd quit school to support their family. After the bank foreclosed on their farm, they relocated near Lexington, where they worked at an inn, and also with horses and cattle. Shortly after they were settled there, their father Lem died. It would ingrain two things into Earl Teater: work as hard as a proverbial horse and hold tight to your money; you never know what life holds around the corner.

After training horses for years and raising his siblings, Earl married his longtime sweetheart, Carrie. In 1925, 20-year-old Earl and Carrie moved to Chicago where Teater took a job as a dealer's rider at a large livery stable on Halsted Street. In the summer, they traveled to Connecticut and New York, working with horses. Teater's skill and renown with horses was growing – as was his family, with the birth of three boys, Earl Jr. (called "Pete"), Louis and Edward. In 1943, the Teaters bought a farm in Harrodsburg, Kentucky, and opened a public training stable. But then Earl received an offer to increase his income, training horses for J. Truman Ward, outside of Nashville. Teater was becoming one of the most successful Saddlebred trainers in the nation – having won multiple championships – and he was just getting warmed up.

From his first shoeing, Wing *had his hooves trimmed monthly and new shoes fitted by one farrier: Earl Smith of Rochester, Michigan. Even after Dodge Stables relocated to Lexington, Kentucky, Smith was flown in to shoe him.* Wing *wore very light shoes in front, which was a testament to his natural gift of snapping his knees higher than his forearm even while at a trot and the rack.*

PHOTO COURTESY OF AMERICAN SADDLEBRED MUSEUM

Whether in the stands or in the stables, Frances Dodge Johnson (seen here with Jimmy in September 1945) was a well-regarded member of the equestrian world. "She is one of the most generous supporters of horse shows and horse events and has been a genuine horse lover since she started riding as a child in pigtails. Today she stands at the top of the field in horse show circles and in the realm of the Saddlebred with the best in all divisions performing in her colors." – Saddle & Bridle, *December 1948.*

PHOTO COURTESY OF JUDY LAVENDAR

After Wallace Bailey died at the end of 1944, Bill Rowan was appointed interim Saddle Horse manager at Dodge Stables. Soon after, Rowan contracted a mild case of polio. Although he continued working at the stables, Frances began looking for a permanent replacement. She and Jimmy began observing Earl Teater, who had an impeccable reputation on the circuit.

In September 1945, after carefully assessing his track record, Frances offered Teater a permanent position as head of the Dodge Stables Saddle division. He was still under contract with the Wards, but J. Truman released Teater from his commitment, encouraging him to accept the new position.

Teater's appointment and the Johnsons' purchase of famed Castleton Farm in Lexington, Kentucky, were announced simultaneously. Now there was a new head of the Saddle division, and the horses and stables would be moving into Bluegrass Country. But Castleton Farm was in major disrepair, so the Johnsons would not begin relocating operations from Rochester to Lexington until two years later, in 1947.

In the meantime, Teater moved his family to Michigan. After he settled in at Dodge Stables, he immediately spotted the 2-year-old *Wing*'s potential. When Teater took *Wing* from the "colt man" (who breaks yearlings) and began to work with him, he realized this dark liver-chestnut colt with the

Wing Commander *and his trainer, Earl Teater.*
PHOTO COURTESY OF KEITH CUPP, *BLUEGRASS HORSEMAN*

Wing Commander *with his blue ribbons, pictured in* LIFE *magazine, October 1954.*

PHOTO COURTESY OF *LIFE* MAGAZINE

An excerpt from the text of Wing's LIFE *story:* "*The greatest stallion in the history of show horse competition is an 11-year-old chestnut champion called* Wing Commander. *Thousands of horse lovers all over the U.S. have cheered the perfection of his five-gaited performance – walk, trot, canter, slow-gaited stepping and the rack. Descended from other champions and trained at Kentucky's Dodge Stables, he is an alert, exceptionally unruffled competitor. Says his trainer, Earl Teater, 'You can load him or ship him everywhere. He'll win as long as we let him compete.'"

big head and the narrow chest had an "unbelievable natural trot." When Teater began to ask for the rack, *Wing* did not disappoint. After only a few weeks of attempts, one morning the gangly colt flew around the large indoor ring at a true rack. Teater said, "He used his legs like no other horse I had ever seen."

Wing Commander began to compete as a 3-year-old, and by then it was like cutting a live wire loose. *Wing* debuted by winning the 1946 3-year-old Five-Gaited stake at the highly regarded Lexington Junior League horse show. He would show – and win – seven times that year before heading to the Chicago International. *Wing* took the Five-Gaited stallion stake there, clinching his title as champion of the year.

Just one year in, 1947, *Wing* took top honors in the prestigious 4-year-old Stallion Stake at Louisville … but he would also taste defeat. *Easter Parade* beat him twice – at the Kentucky State Fair and again at the National Horse Show.

That was the last time *Wing* would lose.

Now working out of Castleton Farm, in 1948 *Wing* and Teater won the Grand Championship at the Kentucky State Fair. Ben Jones, Thoroughbred racehorse trainer of Calumet Farm, compared *Wing's* championship to his recent win in the Kentucky Derby with *Citation*. (*Citation* would later win the Preakness and Belmont to complete the 1948 Triple Crown.) As Jones said, "*Citation* has to be good for only two minutes and *Wing* *had to be conditioned to show upwards of one hour to win his World Grand Champion Five-Gaited title.*"

Earl Teater would also cite *Wing's* winning ways and offer insight into preparing a horse like him for show. In a July 11, 1949, article in the *Lexington Herald-Leader*, Teater said, "Wing Commander *is the greatest I've ever shown, and I've been up on the four or five best horses of the last 15 years. He is the* Citation *of the saddle-horse world, and he's beaten just about as easily … Training a horse for a show is like training a fighter for a bout. You have to keep the horse in condition, watch its feeding, be careful not to let it go stale, don't overwork or underwork it, and know just when it has reached the peak and is ready to show.*"

Walter Wellesley "Red" Smith, that giant of the press box, would also have a thing to say about *Wing Commander*. Smith, a sports columnist for the *New York Herald Tribune*, would later write for *The New York Times* and become the first sports writer to win the Pulitzer Prize for Commentary. But on this night in November 1951, while covering the National Horse Show, he was smitten with *Wing*.

"*Even if you know nothing of conformation, style or saddle horse gaits or horse show manners, you can see at a glance what this stallion's got … At 15.3 hands, he isn't tremendously big, yet, in action, he looks half again the size of anything else in the field. They call him a chestnut but from a loge seat he looks as black as a judge's conscience, with the lights glinting off his arched*

Wing Commander's progeny

The names of the first winners sired by *Wing Commander* appeared on the records of the 1959 Kentucky State Fair Horse Show. Giving due portent of things to come, *Commander's Darling* won the breeders stake and *Commander's Love* won the three-year-old Five-Gaited stake. During the following years *Wing's* descendants triumphed in all divisions. The early champions *Wing* sired are listed at right.

PHOTO COURTESY OF AMERICAN SADDLEBRED MUSEUM

The Five-Gaited champions for four consecutive years:
VALERIE EMERALD (1969)
YORKTOWN (1970-72)

The amateur Five-Gaited champions:
SHEER BLUE (1970)
WING'S FAIR LADY (1971)

The amateur mare stake, ladies' Five-Gaited champion, or ladies' mare division:
TINSEL WINGS (1970)
WING'S FAIR LADY (1971-72)
DREAM LOVER (1970)
WINGED VICTORY (1970)
DREAM LOVER (1971)
WING FLAME (1972)
WING'S ARIA (1971 Kentucky county fair championship)
LIMELIGHT (1972 junior exhibitor mare stake)

Daughters who were winners in other divisions:
TASHI LING – world's fine harness champion (1968-71)
PICTURE PRINCESS – three-gaited division of the
National Three-Year-Old Futurity (1971)

In Saddle & Bridle's *Sire Rating for 1980, seven of* Wing's *sons were in the nation's top 25 stallions:*
FLIGHT TIME
KING DELL
YORKTOWN
WINGMASTER
CHIEF OF GREYSTONE
DANISH COMMANDER
CENTER RING

Also in the top 25 that year were two grandsons, both sired by his son, Wing's Fleet Admiral:
COURAGEOUS ADMIRAL
SUPERIOR ODDS

neck and the blaze and lathered chest making a flashing contrast. He's all fire and power and pride, and as he sweeps around the ring the mink and orchid mob lets go a holler like the crowd at a bull fight or the $2 players on the rail at Jamaica."

Earl knew 1954 would be *Wing's* last year, and he and Frances let up a bit on the 11-year-old stallion. That February, he was used for the first time as a stud to Five-Gaited champion mare, *Sweet Rhythm*. He showed only three times prior to the Kentucky State Fair, and won at all three. His last show appearance was the Chicago International.

By this time, the champion was valued at more than $100,000 – or nearly $1 million today. *Wing Commander* was featured in the October 1954 issue of *LIFE,* America's popular photojournalism magazine. His story, "Best In Blue," pictured *Wing* wearing his 237th first-place blue ribbon – and peering around the corner at his wall, which was plastered with the rest.

Aside from a brief bout with laminitis in 1962 at age 19, *Wing* was enjoying a quiet life as an in-demand sire. But on the morning of January 19, 1969, *Wing's* good health would take a turn for the worse.

Earl Teater immediately called in three veterinarians for a check. They administered medication and treatment, but after only a few hours, the great 26-year-old stallion died. Teater had him buried intact in the horse cemetery at Castleton Farm. There he would join his mother, *Flirtation Walk,* and his father, *Anacacho Shamrock.*

"He was the greatest horse there ever was … this is just like losing a very good friend. There never will be another Wing Commander," Teater said in *The Courier-Journal,* January 21, 1969.

For six consecutive years, *Wing* was crowned the Five-Gaited World's Grand Champion (1948-53) at the Kentucky State Fair, and six times he was considered the number-one sire, from 1963 to 1968. He retired as a senior performer, after grueling campaigns at all the major shows and consecutive victories in the Five-Gaited World's Grand Championship.

Winner of more than 200 championships, it was a feather in *Wing Commander's* mane to be the first horse inducted into the National Horse Show Hall of Fame in December 1985.

Wing sired more than 350 registered Saddlebreds and six world champions. Today, his progeny are stellar competitors in the ring and also produce performers to keep this champion's legacy alive for all time.

Wing Commander accomplished what few could imagine – even surpassing the wildest dreams of his owner, Frances Dodge Van Lennep.

To keep operations running smoothly, Dodge Stables employed many grooms and trainers. From left, some of Dodge Stables' show string and handlers (named in parentheses) at Castleton, 1954: Wing Commander and Showboat *(Gregory Pena);* Meadow Princess *(Joe Pena);* Lover's Lane *(Rudy Pena);* Moon Glitter *(Bob Winkler);* Dream Waltz *(Bethel Ward),* Sparkling Delight *(Judy Johnson, Frances' daughter);* Socko *(Ruben Pena)* and Sparkling Cardinal *(Marion Smith).*

PHOTO COURTESY OF AMERICAN SADDLEBRED MUSEUM

CHAPTER 11

Horse country beckons

Castleton Farm's stately 10,000-square-foot Greek Revival home built in 1840.

Through years of immersing themselves in the horse world, Frances and Jimmy Johnson were drawn to its epicenter, Lexington, Kentucky, and they fell hard for Castleton Farm at 2469 Iron Works Pike Road. This magnificent, historic property, with 14 barns and a 10,000-square-foot house, had been the storied home of highly regarded horses and their owners for centuries.

In 1945, the Johnsons bought it, intending to bring it back to its original glory. They began transitioning breeding operations there in 1947 and started a Standardbred racing stable, but Castleton would not become Dodge Stables' headquarters until 1949. With Sep Palin training the Standardbreds, they bought the foundation sires upon which the farm was built. Their champions kept winning, including the Little Brown Jug and three Hambletonians.

The year between, 1948, would be history-making for Dodge Stables. *Show Boat, Blue Hawaii, Lover's Lane* and *Wing Commander* swept the Kentucky State Fair and the National Horse Show, and won every division of the Five-Gaited stake at Louisville and the junior stake,

Fred Van Lennep on the sulky of Air Record, *a young trotter owned by a friend. He leans over to talk to daughter Rikki, with son John and Frances standing behind, 1959.*

PHOTO COURTESY OF VAN LENNEP FAMILY

Dodge Stables won the Hambletonian Stakes (a major harness race) in 1947 with Hoot Mon, *in 1958 with* Emily's Pride *and in 1963 with* Speedy Scot. *Above: Frances poses with friend O.T. Thompson and the Hambletonian Cup she passed on to the 1959 winner.*

something no other stable had ever done. And to ensure the stable's continued growth, they now had 20 Saddle mares and 38 Standardbred mares of the best bloodlines anywhere.

The Hackney pony division, under Reed Bridgford's watch, also made strides at every competition with *Victory Song, Glenavon Film Star* and *King's Melody*.

As Frances and her horses continued to win accolades, 1948 also marked a season of unraveling. In April, after nearly a decade of marriage, Frances was granted an uncontested divorce from Jimmy, their properties were settled, and she received custody of daughter Judy.

In January 1949, Frances married Frederick Van Lennep, an advertising representative from Philadelphia. His first wife had been active in the horse-show circuit, so their paths had crossed many times. Along with one child each from their first marriages, they would have two children together, Fredericka (Rikki), born in 1951, and John Francis, born in 1952. The children would all grow up riding horses and competing in show rings, many of their mounts trained by Earl Teater.

In November 1954 at the National Horse Show in Madison Square Garden, Dodge Stables took 11 blue ribbons – one for every class shown. Saddlebred stars now included *Meadow Princess* and *Socko*. Retired *Wing's* full sister, *Dream Waltz,* won the blue ribbon at the

Fred and Frances Van Lennep with horse Good Counsel *and trainer Frank Ervin, c. 1958. The Van Lenneps were awarded the Horseman Award from* The Horseman & Fair *magazine in 1969 for the "[immeasurable] impact on all phases of the Standardbred sport over the past quarter-century." When informed of the honor, Frederick Van Lennep said simply, "Give Frances all the credit – it belongs to her."*

PHOTO COURTESY OF CALDWELL FAMILY

1956 Kentucky State Fair in the Five-Gaited division.

Dodge Stables was considered foremost in the country for Saddlebreds, but the Van Lenneps were also excelling with Standardbreds. Frances added several talented trainers to her team, including Wayne "Curly" Smart, Frank Ervin, Ralph Baldwin and Glen Garnsey. The Van Lenneps brought in more champion brood mares, bought the Wolverine Raceway in Michigan, and became major stake owners in The Red Mile racetrack in Kentucky. After years of petitioning the Florida government, in 1964 Frances also opened Pompano Park harness racetrack near Pompano Beach. Her brother, Richard Wilson, managed several of the tracks and became a horse racing authority.

The Van Lenneps owned one of the world's most respected equine enterprises. For Frances, years of weaving together the finest team of horses, trainers and facilities had produced results that were world-class by any measure.

As noted in *The Detroit News*, "It would be easy to write off many of Mrs. Van Lennep's personal accomplishments to the purchasing power of the dollar since the Dodge fortune is vast. However, harness racing and show experts alike say that money alone could never have made her the horsewoman she is. Her husband agrees. "Don't underestimate Frances' ability with horses," he cautions. "She has picked out nearly every good horse she's had."

The nursery barn (above) at Castleton. In 1793, Thoroughbred horse breeder and U.S. Attorney General John B. Breckinridge first settled those 2,467 acres, calling his farm Cabell's Dale. Subsequent owners included his descendant, Confederate General John Breckinridge Castleman (hence "Castleton"), who founded the American Saddlebred Horse Association.

PHOTO COURTESY OF CASTLETON LYONS

Frances atop one of her champion Saddlebreds, Showboat, *1949. Longtime Saddlebred trainer Earl Teater offered insight into Frances as a boss: "Mrs. Van Lennep is the best sport in the business and the best person I've ever worked for." –* Lexington Herald-Leader, *July 11, 1949.*

PHOTO COURTESY OF AMERICAN SADDLEBRED MUSEUM

CHAPTER 12

A legacy lives on

Frances Van Lennep, 1955.

On January 22, 1971, in Pompano Park, Florida, Frances celebrated 22 years of marriage to Frederick Van Lennep in style, donning her first pantsuit. The latest fashion was far different than in her debutante days, but she was always game to be a trendsetter. Friends there with them in Pompano recalled that the couple seemed cheerful and happy.

The next day, while visiting with friends in their oceanfront home in Delray Beach, Frances was stricken with a hemorrhage. Rushed to a hospital in nearby Boca Raton, she fought to stay alive while hundreds who had heard the news waited, hoping and praying. More than 50 employees and friends from Pompano Park offered to donate blood.

She passed away the morning of January 24, just months after she turned 56. Her stepfather, Alfred Wilson, preceded her in death in 1962; her mother, Matilda Dodge Wilson, in 1967.

Services were held at the William R. Hamilton Funeral Home in Detroit, and burial at the Dodge family mausoleum in nearby Woodlawn Cemetery, where her

Frances Dodge's personality was defined by far more than records in the show ring. "Frances was misunderstood by a lot of people because she was so shy," her brother Richard would recall. "At an early age (pictured here at 20), given her place in society and with an over-protective mother, she never really knew who liked her just because of her money. She had it tough, but she was a super person. Frances was fun, loyal, kind, caring and considerate to friends, family and employees alike. In her adult years, every Christmas at Castleton Farm she would send a letter to her employees telling them to pick out something to wear and a toy for each of their children. If they wrote down a bicycle, she'd send them a bicycle. She'd spend thousands of dollars, and she never said no. She was an all-time sweetheart."

PHOTO COURTESY OF CALDWELL FAMILY

father was laid to rest years before. The Wilson mausoleum was adjacent.

Frances left behind her husband, Frederick; her two daughters, Mrs. Judith Johnson Bartlett and Fredericka Dodge Van Lennep; her son, John Francis Van Lennep; a stepson, Hector Van Lennep; a grandson, James William Bartlett; two sisters, Mrs. Winifred Dodge Seyburn and Mrs. Barbara (Wilson) Eccles; and her brother, Richard S. Wilson.

She also left behind an unparalleled legacy.

Her contributions to the horse world were legendary, and in 1973, Frances Van Lennep was inducted into the World's Championship Horse Show Hall of Fame, joining veteran hall of famer, Earl Teater, who had passed away in 1972, a year after Frances.

Posthumously, the two would continue to influence riding and racing industries worldwide. Moving forward, Teater's son, Louis, handled the Saddlebred stallions for Dodge Stables, including one of *Wing's* celebrated sons, *Flight Time*. The dynamic duo – Earl Teater and *Wing Commander* – would continue to flourish through their bloodlines.

Frederick Van Lennep, who had been Frances' partner for

Frances on Blue Hawaii, *c. 1947.*

so many years in building a successful equine enterprise, operated Dodge Stables at its usual pace for several years.

In 1975, he discontinued the Dodge Stables division of Castleton Farm operations. A tribute to the "Dodge Dynasty" in the dispersal sale catalog stated, *"The auctioneer's gavel falling above the last Dodge Stables horse to sell will mark the close of the greatest American Saddle horse stable and breeding farm in history. It was built by Frances Dodge Van Lennep and Earl Teater, and is a monument to their dedication, knowledge, abilities and perseverance."*

Frances Matilda Dodge Van Lennep's legacy will live on through her children and subsequent generations … and through the contributions she made to the future bloodlines and acclaimed histories of the horses she loved so dearly. This kind and generous automotive heiress, this daughter, sister, wife and mother – whose life was marked with triumphs and tragedies alike – took the reins of her life firmly in hand to realize her dreams in and out of the show ring.

About the author

Photo by Sarah Lucander

Karel Bond Lucander is a freelance writer who crafts copy for world-class corporations, advertising agencies, universities and other cultural institutions. Her work has featured interviews with prominent entertainment and sports figures and business leaders. From technical, corporate and institutional literature to travel, leisure and historical feature stories (some appearing in Meadow Brook Magazine), her work spans many genres.

She has received numerous awards for her writing, including ADDY, Business Marketing Association and IABC Silver Quill awards. *Riding on the Edge* is her first published book, and she is grateful for the opportunity to delve into the life of Frances Dodge and Dodge Stables.

When she is not wrestling with words or reading them, Karel enjoys spending time with her family and friends in the mountains and on the beaches of the Carolinas. Born in Detroit, Karel lives in Davidson, North Carolina, with her husband, twins and Yorkshire terriers, Java and Coco.